DISASTERS of Technology

by Sheila Sweeny Higginson

TABLE OF CONTENTS

INTRODUCTION

the *Titanic*

Throughout history, people have been fascinated with travel and exploration. Experts strive to create technologies that will help us go farther and faster. Often, this technology succeeds. We can now ride in trains that travel at record speeds. We are able to send unmanned spacecraft to Mars. Unfortunately, technology sometimes fails, causing disaster to strike.

A giant ship slams into an iceberg and sinks to the bottom of the ocean. An airship bursts into flames as it prepares to land. Millions of people watch as a space shuttle explodes above Earth, killing everyone inside.

the *Hindenburg*

Travel Technology Time Line

1903	1908	1912	1927	1937	1938	1939	1949
Wright Brothers fly at Kitty Hawk	Henry Ford introduces Model-T car	*Titanic* sinks	Charles Lindbergh flies solo across Atlantic Ocean	*Hindenburg* bursts into flames	First passenger plane crosses Atlantic Ocean	Helicopter is invented	First plane flies nonstop around world

the *Challenger*

No one expected the *Titanic*'s first trip across the Atlantic Ocean to end in disaster. The luxury ocean liner had been described as "unsinkable." Before its fiery end, the *Hindenburg* airship had made several safe trips across the Atlantic. Space shuttles had made many successful trips into space before the *Challenger* disaster.

Shocked. Confused. Scared. These were some of the feelings that many people experienced when they heard the news of each disaster.

People wanted to know what went wrong. They wanted to make sure such tragedies wouldn't happen again.

In this book, you'll read more about the *Titanic*, the *Hindenburg*, and the *Challenger*. You'll discover how each was built, what went wrong, and how the disasters changed the way we look at travel and exploration.

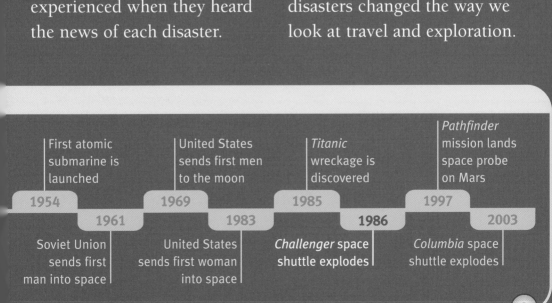

1954	1969	1985	1997
First atomic submarine is launched	United States sends first men to the moon	*Titanic* wreckage is discovered	*Pathfinder* mission lands space probe on Mars

1961	1983	1986	2003
Soviet Union sends first man into space	United States sends first woman into space	*Challenger* space shuttle explodes	*Columbia* space shuttle explodes

THE TITANIC

Titanic means "immense" or "gigantic." It was the perfect name for the biggest and most luxurious (luhg-ZHER-ee-uhs) ship of its time. Construction of the *Titanic* began on March 31, 1909, in a shipyard in Ireland. It took about 14,000 men to build the ocean liner. The **hull**, or main body of the ship, was made with 2,000 one-inch-thick steel plates. Three million rivets, or pieces of metal, held these plates together. The *Titanic* was more than 882 feet long (268.8 meters), as long as the length of about 2 ½ football fields, and weighed 46,328 tons. It was described as a "floating palace." Passengers could swim in a pool, exercise in a gym, or go to a barbershop without leaving the ship. Although this is common on today's cruise ships, it was something special at that time.

the *Titanic* under construction

reading room on the *Titanic*

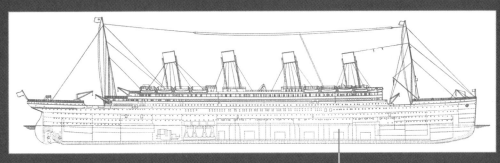

① It took 46,328 tons of steel to build the *Titanic*. One ton equals 2,000 pounds. How many pounds of steel were used to build the *Titanic*?

The engineers who designed the *Titanic* included 16 watertight **compartments**, or spaces. In the event of a flood, the ship's captain could close off any of the compartments with the flip of a switch. Keeping water out of these spaces would keep the ship from sinking. Even if a few of the compartments flooded, the ship would stay afloat. That was the plan, anyway. Because of this design, many considered the *Titanic* to be unsinkable.

Work on the grand ship was completed in March 1912. It was then sailed to England to begin its first ocean voyage.

cross section of the *Titanic*   watertight compartment

IT'S A FACT

The *Titanic*'s first voyage was almost postponed because of a coal shortage. The *Titanic* needed a great deal of coal to run its engines. Other ships gave up their own coal for the *Titanic*. The delay was avoided and the *Titanic* left as planned.

On April 10, 1912, passengers and crew boarded the *Titanic*. The ship set out to sea from Southampton, England, bound for stops in France and Ireland, and then on to New York City. Crowds waved and cheered from the dock.

About 2,200 passengers and crew were on the *Titanic* when it sailed. The passengers included some of the richest people in the world. Also aboard the ship were poor immigrants, looking for a better life in the United States. Passengers traveled in one of three classes: first class, second class, or third class, also known as **steerage**.

Solve This!

2 A ship's speed is measured in *knots*. One knot is equal to 1.15 miles per hour. The average speed of an ocean liner such as the *Titanic* was approximately 19 knots. What was the average speed of these ships in miles per hour?

Passengers stroll along the upper deck of the *Titanic*.

Lady Duff-Gordon

One of the first-class passengers was Lady Duff-Gordon. She was one of the world's richest and most successful businesswomen. She had not planned on taking the *Titanic*. Urgent business in New York required that she take the earliest ship possible.

In second class, Emily Richards enjoyed the night of April 14 on deck. She remembers noticing how cold it was. Richards was traveling with her two children, William, aged 3 years, and George, 10 months. Her mother, sister, and brother were also passengers. Like Lady Duff-Gordon, Emily Richards did not plan to travel on the *Titanic*. She had been transferred from another ship, due to the coal shortage.

Neither Emily Richards nor Lady Duff-Gordon could know of the disaster that lay ahead.

At 11:40 P.M. on April 14, the ship was a few hundred miles away from the coast of Newfoundland, Canada. Most passengers were asleep. From out of the quiet night came a loud ripping or scraping sound. The ship rumbled fiercely. The crew was terrified to discover that the *Titanic* had collided with an iceberg.

E. J. Smith, captain of the *Titanic*

PRIMARY SOURCE

The sinking of the *Titanic* was a major news event. The number of lost and saved passengers was not accurately reported the day after the disaster. That's why the numbers in the headline are not accurate.

"All the News That's Fit to Print."

The New York Times.

TITANIC SINKS FOUR HOURS AFTER HITTING ICEBERG;
866 RESCUED BY CARPATHIA, PROBABLY 1250 PERISH;
ISMAY SAFE, MRS. ASTOR MAYBE, NOTED NAMES MISSING

The Lost Titanic Being Towed Out of Belfast Harbor.

PARTIAL LIST OF THE SAVED.

Solve This!

3 Use the *Titanic* Passengers table to answer the questions.

a. Find the total number of passengers lost.

b. Find the total number of passengers saved.

c. Which class lost approximately 3/4 of its passengers?

Titanic Passengers

	Total	Lost	Saved
1st Class	325	122	203
2nd Class	285	167	118
3rd Class	706	528	178
Crew	890	678	212

Water flooded into several of the ship's compartments. When it became clear that the ship was taking on water and starting to sink, the crew prepared to **evacuate**. The plan was to get everyone into the lifeboats as quickly as possible. But there were not enough lifeboats to hold everyone on the ship. Some people panicked, grabbed anything they hoped would keep them afloat, and jumped overboard.

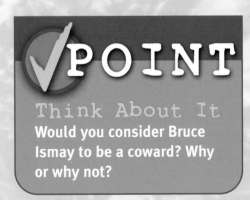

Lifeboats carried survivors from the *Titanic*. Many of the boats were launched carrying fewer than their 65-passenger capacity.

The terror the passengers and crew felt is hard to imagine. At about 2:20 A.M. on April 15, the *Titanic* split in two and sank. It took nearly two hours more for the first rescue ship to arrive. The *Carpathia* picked up about 700 survivors. About 1,500 people died, many by drowning or freezing to death in the icy water.

The captain of the *Titanic*, Edward J. Smith, chose to go down with the ship. Bruce Ismay, the president of the company that owned the *Titanic*, was also aboard. He chose to escape in a lifeboat.

✓ **POINT**

Think About It
Would you consider Bruce Ismay to be a coward? Why or why not?

Numbers in the News

The 1997 movie *Titanic* was very popular—and a huge moneymaker. It made more than $600,000,000 in the United States. That was more money than any movie had made before. The total rose to more than $1,835,000,000 after the movie was shown around the world.

Could this disaster have been avoided? That night, other ships had sent out warnings of icebergs in the area. But the *Titanic* crew was too busy to pay attention. Some say the *Titanic* was moving too fast in dangerous waters. Even if the iceberg could not have been avoided, many more people would have survived if there had been enough lifeboats.

It was the *Titanic* disaster that brought about several changes in shipping **regulations**. These new rules required that a ship have enough lifeboats to hold every person on board. The International Ice Patrol was formed to help ships traveling in icy areas. And all ships have to have someone listening for radio warnings and distress calls, 24 hours a day.

For more than 70 years, the wreckage of the *Titanic* remained unexplored at the bottom of the sea. Scientists believed they could discover why the great ship sank by examining the wreckage. Several teams attempted, unsuccessfully, to find it.

On September 1, 1985, a team of scientists, led by oceanographer Dr. Robert Ballard, found the *Titanic*. It was in two pieces on the ocean floor. Many items from the ship were later recovered, or **salvaged**. But more importantly, scientists were finally able to study the wreckage and form ideas about the cause of the disaster.

Initially, it was believed that an iceberg sliced through the ship's hull. But scientists did not find a huge gash in the hull. Some scientists think that the hull's steel was too weak to handle the frigid

Solve This!

A The *Titanic* was found 4,000 meters below sea level. One meter equals 3.28 feet. How many feet below sea level was the *Titanic* found?

temperatures of the Atlantic Ocean. Perhaps when the ship crashed into the iceberg, the hull simply split open. Still others think the steel panels ripped apart at the seams because of weak rivets.

Today, the *Titanic* remains undersea. Dr. Ballard placed a plaque on the ship as a memorial to those who died.

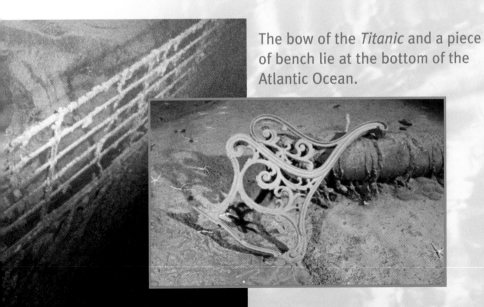

The bow of the *Titanic* and a piece of bench lie at the bottom of the Atlantic Ocean.

THE HINDENBURG

the *Hindenburg*

Have you ever seen a blimp in the sky? If you have, then you've seen an airship known as a **dirigible** (DER-uh-juh-buhl). A dirigible is a cigar-shaped, gas-filled balloon that is powered by a motor and can be steered. Now imagine an airship at least four times longer than a blimp, and you'll have some idea how big the German airship *Hindenburg* was.

The *Hindenburg* was more than 803 feet (240.9 meters) long. That's about as long as 20 large school buses in a row. It was the largest aircraft ever flown. The hull was made from a metal frame covered with cloth. Inside the hull were large compartments filled with a gas that is lighter than air. This gas is what made the airship rise into the sky.

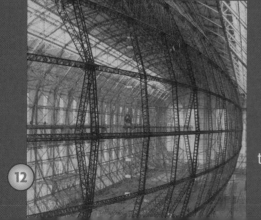

the *Hindenburg* under construction

The gas used in the *Hindenburg* was hydrogen (HIGH-druh-juhn). Hydrogen is a very **flammable** gas. That means that it catches fire easily and burns quickly. The *Hindenburg* was first designed to use helium (HEE-lee-uhm), which is a much safer gas. Helium was not available in Germany at the time, so the *Hindenburg* was redesigned to use hydrogen instead.

The *Hindenburg* was also designed to carry passengers. In the 1930s, the farthest airplanes could travel was about 2,470 miles (3,970 kilometers). They could carry only small amounts of weight. They weren't really an option for travelers who wanted to cross the Atlantic Ocean.

Ocean liners such as the *Titanic* could take about a week to cross. But an airship like the *Hindenburg* could cross the Atlantic in only three days.

Solve This!

5 Look at the table. How many more hours would it take to cross the Atlantic in the *Hindenburg* than in the *Concorde*?

Crossing the Atlantic	
Method of Transportation	**Duration of Trip**
Titanic (estimated)	7 days
Hindenburg	3 days
Spirit of St. Louis (first plane to make a nonstop flight across the Atlantic)	33 hours
Concorde (passenger jet that could travel faster than the speed of sound)	4 hours

As with the *Titanic*, the *Hindenburg* offered passengers a stylish way to travel. Plush carpets covered the floors. Fancy curtains hung on the windows. The private rooms, called staterooms, were small. But there were also larger rooms on the *Hindenburg* where people could gather.

There was a reading and writing room where people could sit and write postcards. A piano lounge provided entertainment. Dinners were prepared by professional chefs and served on fine china. A wall of windows gave people a spectacular view of the world below.

Traveling in style on an airship was not cheap. A one-way ticket on the *Hindenburg* cost $400.00. That was a great deal of money at the time. A new car cost about that much. But many felt the trip was worth the money.

A Nazi Symbol

In the days of the *Hindenburg*, Adolf Hitler and the Nazi (NAHT-see) Party ruled Germany. The airship was decorated with swastikas, which were symbols of Nazi power. Thousands of small Nazi flags were dropped from the *Hindenburg* when it flew over Germany.

All of the *Hindenburg's* flights in 1936 were sold out. One passenger said that the ride was so smooth it felt like he was being carried on the arms of angels.

Solve This!

6 The *Hindenburg* had a volume of 7,062,100 cubic feet. An average-sized classroom has a volume of about 7,000 cubic feet. Approximately how many classrooms could have fit inside the *Hindenburg*?

A passenger uses the sink in a stateroom of the *Hindenburg*.

Fine dining was offered to passengers on the *Hindenburg's* flights.

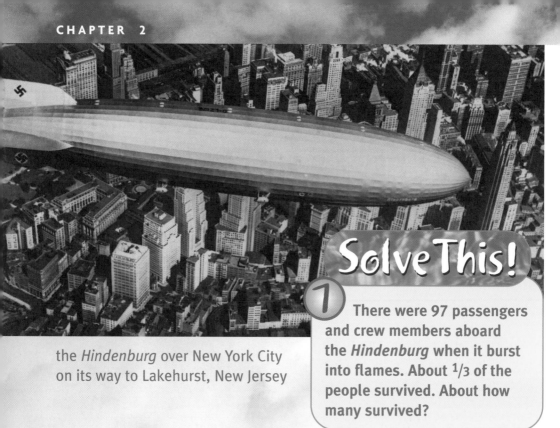

the *Hindenburg* over New York City on its way to Lakehurst, New Jersey

Solve This!

(1) There were 97 passengers and crew members aboard the *Hindenburg* when it burst into flames. About 1/3 of the people survived. About how many survived?

On May 3, 1937, crew and passengers boarded the *Hindenburg* in Frankfurt, Germany. They were headed for Lakehurst, New Jersey. As they approached New Jersey, passengers enjoyed a scenic view of New York City. They could see the Empire State Building and the Statue of Liberty. They could even see a baseball game at Ebbets Field.

The *Hindenburg*'s landing was delayed because of bad weather. Hours later than planned, the crew prepared to land at Lakehurst. But the landing never happened. About 200 feet above the ground, the airship caught fire. Within seconds, the ship was in flames. As shocked witnesses looked on, passengers and crew jumped. The *Hindenburg* crashed to the ground. It had taken only 37 seconds to destroy the mighty *Hindenburg*. Only the metal frame was left.

PRIMARY SOURCE

The crowd of shocked onlookers at the *Hindenburg* disaster included news reporters. Herbert Morrison, a reporter for a Chicago radio station, could not hide the emotions he felt. His report became famous and is still remembered today:

"It's crashing. It's crashing terrible. Oh, my... get out of the way, please. It's bursting into flames. And it's falling on the mooring mast. All the folks agree this is terrible, one of the worst catastrophes in the world. Oh, the flames, four or five hundred feet in the sky, it's a terrific crash, ladies and gentlemen. The smoke and the flames now and the frame is crashing to the ground, not quite to the mooring mast. Oh, the humanity and all the passengers."

Both the United States and German governments investigated the tragedy. Some people believed that a bomb had been planted on the *Hindenburg* in an act of **sabotage** (SA-buh-tahzh). They thought someone might have destroyed the German airship in order to damage Adolf Hitler's Nazi government.

But investigations found no proof of wrongdoing. Instead, they suspected that the cause of the fire was a hydrogen leak. They thought that a spark, caused by static electricity, probably ignited the hydrogen.

Many scientists today disagree with that theory. They don't believe a hydrogen leak could have caused the fire, because many eyewitnesses had reported seeing colorful flames. Flames from burning hydrogen are not very visible.

Robert Bain, a former NASA scientist, believes the cause of the disaster lies in the fabric that covered the *Hindenburg*'s hull. The chemical used to stretch and waterproof the fabric was similar to what is used to make rocket fuel. When the *Hindenburg* flew through a thunderstorm, it picked up static electricity.

Bain believes that a spark from the static electricity could have set the airship's fabric skin on fire.

Whatever the cause, the crash of the *Hindenburg* led to the end of airship travel. By the late 1940s, the development of the jet engine led to faster and more reliable airplanes. The era of airship travel was over.

Airship travel was replaced by faster and more reliable airplanes.

Smoke and flames rise from the *Hindenburg*.

THE CHALLENGER

Humans have been fascinated by space for thousands of years. But it wasn't until the late 1950s and 1960s that developments in technology brought the world into "the space age." The U.S. government developed a space program, run by the National Aeronautics and Space Administration (NASA). Russia developed a space program as well. Then in July of 1969, U.S. astronauts walked on the moon—a major landmark in the history of space exploration.

Since then, space scientists have continued to develop technology for exploration. In 1977, NASA remodeled an airplane to carry a glider on top of it. While the plane was in flight, the glider was released. The glider floated smoothly for a while and then landed on the desert floor. This experiment led to the development of the Space Transportation System, or space shuttle. NASA believed that one day the space shuttle would carry passengers to space stations, where they could live and work.

Rocket Boosters

Fuel Tank

Orbiter

USA

NASA Discovery

A space shuttle is 122.17 feet long (37.24 meters). That's a little smaller than many commercial passenger airplanes. At about 165,000 pounds (74,842 kilograms), the shuttle weighs about as much as 16 school buses! The space shuttle has three main parts: an orbiter, two rocket boosters, and a fuel tank. The astronauts travel inside the orbiter. The orbiter is covered with heat-proof tiles. These tiles protect the craft from burning up when it reenters Earth's **atmosphere**. You might have heard or read news reports that use the term "space shuttle" to talk about the orbiter. But the orbiter is just a piece of the entire space shuttle.

The shuttle's fuel tank and rocket boosters give the shuttle the enormous push it needs to escape Earth's atmosphere and the pull of **gravity**. After the rocket boosters and the fuel tank do their job, they fall off. Then the orbiter begins its **orbit** around Earth.

Solve This!

8 Use the graph to answer the following questions.

a. In which 10-year period did costs double?

b. In which 10-year period did costs decrease?

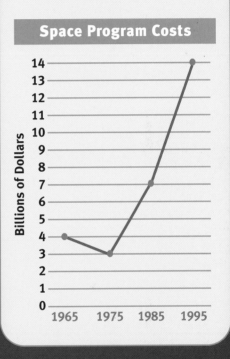

Space Program Costs

During the launch, some astronauts are in the uppermost part of the orbiter. This is called the flight deck. The captain and pilot control the mission from the flight deck. The area just below the flight deck is called mid-deck. This is where the astronauts sleep, eat, and use the bathroom. Mid-deck is also where the hatch is. The hatch is a door that astronauts use to leave the shuttle while in space.

The orbiter also contains a very large cargo bay. It holds such things as satellites and lab equipment. Astronauts sometimes work on scientific missions inside the cargo bay.

Solve This!

9 Use the pie chart to answer these questions.

a. What kind of training takes 150 hours?

b. The pie chart shows the approximate total number of hours that an astronaut must train. Suppose an astronaut completed medical, robotic arm, and language training. How many more hours of training does he or she have left?

Approximate Number of Training Hours of a Space Station Astronaut

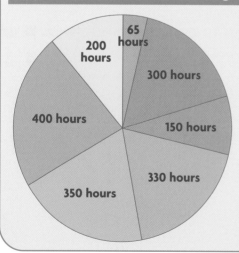

■ = medical training
■ = language training
■ = science experiment training
■ = learning U.S. space station systems
■ = learning Russian space station systems
■ = learning to do spacewalks (300 hrs. in U.S. spacesuits; 100 hrs. in Russian spacesuits)
□ = robotic arm training

Every two years, about 4,000 people apply to be astronauts. NASA selects only 20 of them for training. These people are already test pilots, scientists, physicians, or engineers. They have to be in excellent physical condition. And they have to know how to work well with others.

In 1985, NASA formed the Teacher in Space program. It would choose one teacher to join the crew of the space shuttle. From the more than

✓ POINT

Picture It

Reread page 22. Draw a picture of what you think the inside of a space shuttle looks like.

11,000 teachers who applied for the position, NASA chose Christa McAuliffe. Her role was to teach lessons and share her experiences with students on Earth while she was on the space shuttle *Challenger.* McAuliffe called her adventure "The Ultimate Field Trip." She trained with the astronauts for 114 hours. When launch time came, she was ready.

THEY MADE A DIFFERENCE

Christa McAuliffe never thought NASA would choose her because she was just an average person. Apparently, NASA thought she was a pretty special teacher. McAuliffe taught social studies in a New Hampshire high school. Her students said she made her lessons come alive.

On January 28, 1986, NASA prepared for the shuttle's launch from the Kennedy Space Center in Florida. A crowd nearby waited in the cold weather to watch the launch. Millions of people watched the launch on televisions at work, home, or school. The countdown began. At exactly 11:38 A.M., the *Challenger* blasted off. People cheered.

But joy quickly turned to horror. The shuttle was about 11 miles above Earth when it

the *Challenger* crew

burst into flames. One of the *Challenger*'s fuel tanks had exploded. Witnesses, including Christa McAuliffe's class, were shocked and saddened. All seven people on board the *Challenger* died. The U.S. space program had never seen a worse disaster.

The space shuttle *Challenger* was launched from Kennedy Space Center. It exploded just minutes after takeoff.

The *Challenger* had already flown nine successful missions. What had caused its 10th trip to end in disaster? Looking for clues, NASA recovered giant pieces of the *Challenger* that had fallen into the sea.

a piece of *Challenger* wreckage that was recovered

PRIMARY SOURCE

Ronald Reagan was the U.S. president at the time of the *Challenger* disaster. He spoke to the nation after the tragedy. Here is part of his speech.

"I know it is hard to understand, but sometimes painful things like this happen. It's all part of the process of exploration and discovery. It's all part of taking a chance.... The future doesn't belong to the fainthearted; it belongs to the brave.... Nothing ends here; our hopes and our journeys continue."

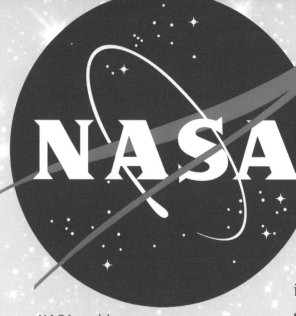

NASA emblem

The investigation found that two small parts of the shuttle caused the disaster. The parts—called O-rings—were part of the rocket boosters. The O-rings are supposed to seal in the hot gases that are created during ignition. But because of the cold temperatures that morning, the O-rings failed. The super-hot gases leaked and ignited the fuel tank, causing it to explode.

The investigation also laid blame on NASA. The night before the *Challenger*'s launch, engineers from the company that made the O-rings spoke to NASA staff. They told them that they were afraid the O-rings wouldn't work in such cold weather. After some discussion, NASA decided to go ahead with the launch.

The *Challenger* disaster had a great impact on NASA. Engineers fixed the O-rings and created an escape system for space shuttle crews. NASA decided that safety was far more important than keeping schedules. They created new guidelines about conditions that might make a launch unsafe. They put the shuttle program on hold for two-and-a-half years.

the crew of the *Columbia*

Then in 1988, the space shuttle program began again with the *Discovery*. After it completed its mission successfully, NASA was encouraged. The space shuttle program continued and went well—until February 1, 2003. On that day, seven astronauts on the space shuttle *Columbia* were heading back to Earth. They were all killed when *Columbia* burst into flames. Damage to the orbiter's left wing was likely the problem. Once again, the nation mourned the lost astronauts. Once again, the space shuttle program was put on hold.

the *Columbia* explosion

a piece of the wreckage of the space shuttle *Columbia*

Solve This!

10 The *Columbia* was traveling very fast when it burst into flames. At the speed it was moving, it could have traveled about 12,000 miles in one hour. How far could it have traveled in one minute?

CONCLUSION

Technology for travel and exploration has improved our world in many ways. We can travel thousands of miles in a few hours. Weather satellites in space help us to predict dangerous weather.

Sometimes technology fails. Sometimes those failures cause disasters, as they did with the *Titanic*, the *Hindenburg*, and the *Challenger*. But we almost always learn from such disasters. As President Reagan said after the *Challenger* disaster, "It's all part of the process of exploration and discovery."

Satellite data was used to create this computer-generated image of Earth.

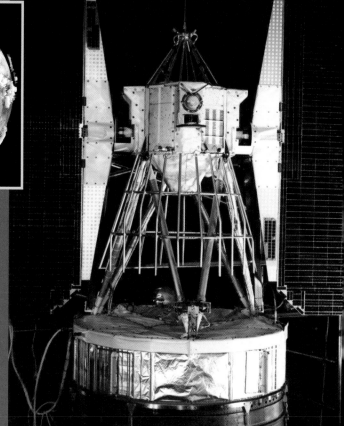

a weather satellite

a magnified look at the soil near the *Opportunity*'s landing site

An artist's conception shows the Mars Exploration Rover on the surface of Mars.

These disasters haven't stopped us from exploring. In January 2004, the unmanned spacecraft *Opportunity* landed on Mars. The Mars Exploration Rover was launched onto the surface of Mars from the *Opportunity*. This success led many to dream about sending people to Mars. Meanwhile, others search for faster, better ways to travel on Earth. Some explore the bottoms of the deepest oceans to uncover Earth's mysteries. Risky? Yes. But as President Reagan said about the *Challenger* crew, people like these are "pulling us into the future, and we'll continue to follow them…."

Solve This!

ANSWERS

① page 5:
92,656,000 pounds

② page 6:
21.85 miles per hour

③ page 8:
a. 1,495 passengers
b. 711 passengers
c. 3rd class

④ page 11:
13,120 feet below sea level

⑤ page 13:
It would take the *Hindenburg* 68 more hours than the *Concorde* to cross the Atlantic.

⑥ page 15:
about 1,009 classrooms

⑦ page 16:
about 32 people survived

⑧ page 21:
a. spending doubled between 1985 and 1995
b. spending decreased between 1965 and 1975

⑨ page 22:
a. science experiment training
b. 1,230 more hours of training

⑩ page 27:
200 miles

GLOSSARY

atmosphere   (AT-muh-sfeer) the mixture of gases that surrounds Earth (page 21)

compartment   (kuhm-PAHRT-muhnt) one of the separate sections into which a space is divided (page 5)

dirigible   (DER-uh-juh-buhl) an airship that is lifted by gases (page 12)

evacuate   (ih-VA-kyoo-wayt) to leave a place in an organized way due to an emergency (page 8)

flammable   (FLA-muh-buhl) capable of easily catching fire (page 13)

gravity   (GRA-vuh-tee) a force that pulls objects toward Earth (page 21)

hull   (HUHL) the main body of a ship (page 4)

orbit   (OR-biht) the path an object follows in circling a planet or the Sun (page 21)

regulation   (re-gyuh-LAY-shuhn) a rule that must be followed according to law (page 10)

sabotage   (SA-buh-tahzh) the act of damaging something on purpose (page 18)

salvage   (SAL-vihj) to recover items from a wreck (page 11)

steerage   (STEER-ihj) the section on a ship for people paying the lowest fares (page 6)

INDEX